The
Story
of
Oil

How It
Changed
the
World

The World Transformed

BY KATHERINE MCLEAN BREVARD

Content Adviser:
Warren Hildebrandt, Former Manager of Natural Resources—
Worldwide, Getty Oil Company

Reading Adviser:
Alexa L. Sandmann, Ed.D., Professor of Literacy,
College and Graduate School of Education, Health, and
Human Services, Kent State University

Compass Point Books
151 Good Counsel Drive
P.O. Box 669
Mankato, MN 56002-0669

Printed in the United States of America in North Mankato, Minnesota.
092009
005618CGS10

Editor: Jennifer Fretland VanVoorst
Designer: Ashlee Suker
Media Researcher: Eric Gohl
Library Consultant: Kathleen Baxter
Production Specialist: Jane Klenk

Image Credits: Alamy/Photos 12, 14; Capstone Studio/Karon Dubke, 49;
Corbis, 23; Corbis/Bettmann, 8, 12, 13, 21, 31, 32, 41; Corbis/Underwood &
Underwood, 15; Getty Images Inc./Hulton Archive/Edwin Levick, 19; Getty
Images Inc./Hulton Archive/FPG, 40; Getty Images Inc./Hulton Archive/
Harold M. Lambert, 38; Getty Images Inc./Newsmakers/Texas Energy
Museum, 27, 30; Getty Images Inc./Stock Montage, 24; Getty Images Inc./
Time Life Pictures/Bill Pierce, 43; Getty Images Inc./Time Life Pictures/
Mansell, 18; Getty Images Inc./Visuals Unlimited/Dr. Marli Miller, 10;
Library of Congress, 1, 9, cover; Mary Evans Picture Library, 5, 34; National
Archives and Records Administration, 36; Shutterstock/Armin Rose, 53;
Shutterstock/Forest Badger, 50; Shutterstock/Henryk Sadura, 52; Shutter
stock/oorka, 55; Shutterstock/photobank.kiev.ua, 44; Shutterstock/TebNad,
57; The Granger Collection, New York, 29; Wikipedia/United States Army
Corps of Engineers/Jonas Jordan, 46.

This book was manufactured with paper containing
at least 10 percent post-consumer waste.

Library of Congress Cataloging-in-Publication Data
Brevard, Katherine McLean.
  The story of oil: how it changed the world / by Katherine McLean Brevard.
     p. cm. — (The world transformed)
  Includes bibliographical references and index.
  ISBN 978-0-7565-4314-3 (library binding)
  1. Petroleum—Juvenile literature. I. Title.
  TN870.3.B74 2010
  303.48'3—dc22   2009034859

Visit Compass Point Books on the Internet at *www.compasspointbooks.com*
or e-mail your request to *custserv@compasspointbooks.com*

TABLE OF CONTENTS

Chapter 1

THE EARLY DAYS OF OIL

I t has created businesses that are richer and more powerful than many of the nations of the world. It has caused wars that have resulted in great suffering and strife for millions of people. It fuels not only our automobiles, but the economy of our planet as well. For the past century, in many ways, oil has ruled the world.

Yet roughly 150 years ago there was no oil industry and there never had been, although people had used oil for thousands of years. In the 16th and 17th centuries, American colonists collected petroleum from pools, where it had risen to the surface, and they put it on their skin to treat arthritis and rheumatism. During the Middle Ages, Christian Crusaders poured oil into wooden boxes that they set aflame and hurled in massive catapults, as well as in handheld slings, at their Islamic enemies. And when invaders were scaling the walls of castles, defenders famously poured boiling oil down on them. Boiling oil was first used as a weapon by Jews who were defending their town against Roman invaders early in

More than 2,000 years ago, the ancient Greeks lit their homes using oil lamps.

the first century.

More than 500 years before that, Persians used oil on their arrows to fire flaming projectiles at opposing armies. At about the same time, Chinese burned petroleum in their

The Story of OIL

OILED MUMMIES

The ancient Egyptians sometimes used an oil tar made from petroleum as part of the process for making mummies. One of the final parts of the mummification process was to wash the body and wrap it in as many as 35 layers of linen that had been soaked in resins and oils. This gave the mummy's skin a blackened appearance.

The term mummification comes from the Arabic word *mummiya*, which means bitumen, a petroleum-derived substance. The oil that was used to make bitumen and then to make mummies was transported to Egypt from the Dead Sea, where petroleum was found floating on the surface of the water. The ancient Egyptians used bitumen to make mummies out of people when they died. They also made mummies of their favorite pets, including dogs, monkeys, gazelles, and cats, so they could take the animals with them into the afterlife.

lamps. King Nebuchadnezzar used it to make mortar for bricks in the famous Hanging Gardens of Babylon and to line pipes that carried water to plants in the gardens. During Babylonian times, entire cities were built using it in the foundations of buildings. What's more, for nearly 6,500 years Middle Eastern seamen applied it to the outside of their houses and boats as waterproofing and to repair leaks. The method was called caulking and it is still used to waterproof some boats today. In parts of the world, sailors were called "tars" because their clothes were deeply stained with oil tar from caulking on their boats and ships.

Yet the first use of oil we know of is far older still. More than 20,000 years ago, Stone Age hunters used a black petroleum substance called bitumen to attach and hold flint arrowheads to their arrows.

Before the mid-1800s, however, no more than a few hundred gallons of petroleum were collected around the world each year. Then in 1849 Abraham Gesner, an inventor in Nova Scotia, Canada, discovered how to refine kerosene. By heating crude oil, he could separate it into various lighter fuels, including kerosene, diesel, and gasoline. At that time, whale oil was the chief source of light and heat for homes. But Gesner had found that kerosene burned longer and more cleanly than whale oil, and it provided a stronger, more consistent, and more reliable light. It also was far less expensive than whale oil. Heating a small house with whale oil cost more than $10 a month. The same home could be heated with kerosene for less than $10 a year. Within a few years of Gesner's discovery, kerosene lamps forced whale oil lamps off the market.

Gesner expanded his business to the United States in 1854. He created the North American Kerosene Gas Light Company in Newton Creek, New York, and it was soon making more than 5,000 gallons (19,000 liters) of kerosene each day. Five years later, 34 new American companies were each selling $5 million worth of kerosene annually. Many

Home Light Oil Company bragged about its ability to light the world in a 19th century advertisement.

A 19th century advertisement for kerosene shows the Statue of Liberty holding a kerosene lantern.

ambitious men saw the large profits to be made. The rush to find petroleum—and to make gigantic fortunes—had begun.

Edwin L. Drake was one of the fortune seekers. He read a newspaper article saying that salt miners near Titusville,

Pennsylvania, had complained that their digs were being ruined by oil seeping up out of the ground. Drake had worked as a hotel clerk, a dry goods salesman, and a railway express agent before becoming a conductor on the New Haven Railroad. He had no technical expertise or knowledge of petroleum or geology. But he was able, as an employee, to travel for free on the New Haven Railroad, so he went to Titusville to investigate the facts behind the article. He hired William A. Smith, a salt well driller and blacksmith, to be

Crude oil, which is found underground in rock formations, sometimes bubbles up to the surface, but it is usually found by drilling.

his oil driller. "Uncle Billy," as Smith was called by almost everyone who knew him, was paid $2.50 a week.

In August 1859, Drake and Smith began digging at a place where oil bubbled up out of a freshwater spring. The water ruined their dig, so they decided to drill. Smith built a battering ram that he used to pound metal piping into the ground. But the piping struck bedrock and stopped 39 feet (12 meters) below the surface. Drake then drove hollow cast-iron pipe down to the bedrock. Using a steam engine, he drilled inside the pipe.

On Saturday, August 27, the men pulled their tools out of the well and went home as usual. When Smith visited the well Sunday morning, he saw dark fluid floating on the water near

HOW DOES OIL FORM?

Oil is a fossil fuel. Along with coal and natural gas, it was formed millions of years ago from the remains of plants and microscopic organisms. Sediment covered the dead matter and formed into rock. More layers of rock formed above, and the weight of the rock created pressure that turned the organic remains into coal, oil, and natural gas, our three main fossil fuels.

the top of the pipe. When Drake arrived at the site on Monday, he found Smith standing guard over several large wooden barrels of oil. In 1859 oil was selling for more than $20 a

Edwin Drake (right) in front of the oil well he drilled, the nation's first

barrel, and a barrel held 42 gallons (160 liters). At the time, bread cost 3 cents a loaf, and milk was a nickel a gallon.

News of Drake's success in finding "black gold," as it was called, quickly spread. Hundreds, then thousands, of men came to Pennsylvania seeking their fortune. Many wells were drilled in the area. The large amount of crude oil the wells produced was refined to provide inexpensive lamp light and lubrication for industrial machines, which were becoming ever more essential to modern civilization. So many men staked claims to drill that the oil fields quickly

By the late 1800s, petroleum was being marketed as the key ingredient in various health and beauty products.

became covered by forests of wells with their tall, treelike derricks. It was common to see hundreds of derricks in one area, pouring out plumes of oil smoke that darkened the skies.

Towns sprang up almost overnight near the drilling sites. Pithole City was one of these towns. It was settled in 1865, and within a year it had 15,000 residents, more than 50 hotels, many boarding houses, saloons, and a post office that handled more than 10,000 letters a day. Many of the

Drake's drilling site quickly became a forest of derricks. Today fewer derricks are needed to pump oil—only about one per 40 acres (16 hectares).

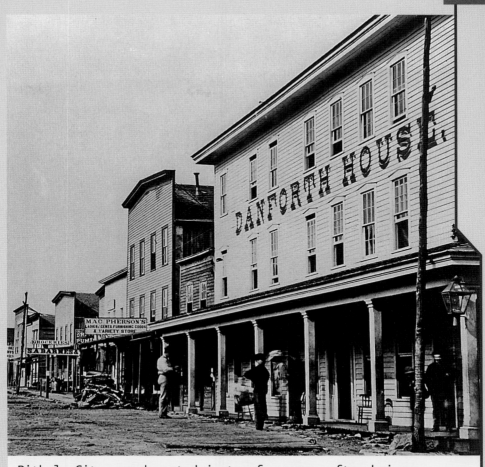

Pithole City was deserted just a few years after being established; today no trace of the city remains.

letters ended up in the "dead letter" office because the fortune hunters left Pithole City quickly, often without giving their next addresses.

In mid-1865, Pennsylvania oil wells were producing more than 6,000 barrels a day. Before the end of the year, however, fewer than 2,000 barrels a day could be eked from the wells. No one could have known in advance that this

The Story of **OIL**

BAKU

The world's first oil well was not in Pennsylvania. It was drilled in 1847 at Baku in modern-day Azerbaijan on the Caspian Sea. Hundreds of wells were quickly drilled after oil was found there, and Baku soon became known as the Black City. By the 1860s, Baku was producing about 90 percent of the world's oil. Today, long after the Pennsylvania wells dried up, Baku is still a major producer of oil.

would happen—that the wells would dry up—especially so fast. Two years later, only a trickle of oil could be pumped from any of the wells in the area. Pithole City was deserted, a ghost town. A section of "oil rich" land that had sold for $2 million in 1865 was auctioned for $4.37 in 1867.

Drake's fortune dried up as the wells did. He is now called the father of the modern petroleum industry, and he is credited with the invention of the drive pipe still used today. Had he patented his invention, he might have lived a life of comfort and wealth. Instead he died penniless in 1880.

Chapter 2

MONOPOLIZING THE MARKET

By the late 1800s, Americans had come to regard kerosene heating and lighting as necessities. Wealth was guaranteed for any man who could quickly find, extract, and refine petroleum.

Nineteen-year-old John D. Rockefeller started a food-shipping company in Cleveland, Ohio, in 1858. His business specialized in pork, salt, and wheat. The demand for these staples for soldiers fighting in the Civil War, which began three years later, soon made Rockefeller a wealthy man. In the fall of 1863, the railroad reached Cleveland, linking it to the oil-rich regions of Pennsylvania. Within months dozens of oil refineries sprang up along the city's railroad tracks.

Realizing that the war, and the strong demand for the food products he shipped, would not last forever, Rockefeller decided that his future lay in oil. He knew there was a high demand for it in America's rapidly expanding urban areas. In 1864, when he was 25, Rockefeller bought his first oil refinery, an already profitable business, by outbidding his partner.

In just two years, annual sales of Rockefeller Kerosene reached the enormous sum of $2 million.

Rockefeller decided it would be to his benefit to stabilize the price of oil. He bought ships to transport kerosene from Cleveland to Chicago and elsewhere in the Midwest by way of the Great Lakes. He also bought railroad tanker cars to take crude oil to warehouses and refineries in New York. In

John D. Rockefeller was photographed in 1865, one year after buying his first oil refinery.

A Standard Oil refinery was built on a wharf to allow for easy shipping by water.

addition he purchased hundreds of thousands of acres of forestland to ensure an abundant supply of white oak trees with which to make barrels.

Rockefeller was determined to protect his business from economic uncertainty and to eliminate competition. To do this, he considered it essential to free his business from the grip of the most powerful industrial force in 1870s America—the railroads. Almost all businesses needed the railroad companies for rapid transportation of their products and supplies. So they paid whatever shipping price the railroads charged. Rockefeller decided to reverse the situation.

For this monumental task, he hired Henry Flagler, who would quickly become Rockefeller's most trusted business associate. Flagler had previously made and lost a fortune distilling whiskey. He was an outgoing, highly social man—the perfect counterpart to the sullen, standoffish Rockefeller.

Rockefeller formed Standard Oil Company in January 1870. He made it Flagler's responsibility, as the company's secretary, to negotiate the all-important railroad shipping rates. Flagler had a very strong bargaining position in dealing with the railroads. Standard Oil dominated the oil industry and was the railroad companies' largest customer. The company shipped more than a million barrels of crude oil and kerosene each year. Its largest competitor shipped less than a quarter of that amount.

Flagler was ruthless in negotiating with the railroads. Standard Oil, he told them, would not pay the same price that other customers did. The Standard Oil account was such a big part of the railroads' business that Flagler could force the railroad owners to offer the shipping price he wanted.

Rockefeller and Flagler didn't care how other business owners, their own competitors, or the American public viewed Standard Oil's business practices. Rockefeller undercut the prices of other oil companies so much that the competitors could not make a profit. Many business owners were left with only two options: Sell their companies to Standard Oil or go

Standard Oil paid lower rates for shipping by rail,
which enabled the company to dominate the oil industry.

broke. By early 1872, Standard Oil had bought and absorbed
21 oil-refining firms in the Cleveland area alone. Rockefeller
had been in the oil business less than 10 years, but already he
had become the richest man in the United States.

The Story of **OIL**

The average American in the 1870s made $5 to $10 a week. A good wage was $500 a year. John D. Rockefeller's personal wealth in the 1870s was outlandishly large. He was wealthier than Microsoft Corporation founder Bill Gates would become in the 1990s. (In today's money, Rockefeller would be worth more than $250 billion, which dwarfs the fortunes of all present-day billionaires.)

Rockefeller's enormous wealth, cold personality, bullying business tactics, and personal ruthlessness earned him the nickname "robber baron." The term was used to describe many wealthy businessmen of the time who were believed to dominate their industries through unfair business practices. And Rockefeller did indeed dominate his industry. By 1879

REFINING OIL

Oil refining separates crude oil into various substances. The oldest and most common method is distilling. In this process, crude oil is heated until it turns into a vapor. As it cools, it is separated into various oil products, such as gasoline, jet fuel, diesel, and asphalt. Newer processes use chemicals to break down oil into different substances.

Standard Oil controlled more than 90 percent of the oil refinery business in the United States.

Rockefeller was strongly disliked and feared by the American public. His overwhelming wealth and power made many people worry that America's free-enterprise system was in danger of disappearing. In 1882 he organized the Standard Oil Trust, a legal mechanism that allowed him to create an almost complete monopoly of the oil industry.

As the Pennsylvania oil wells began to dry up, the center of oil production shifted west to newly discovered fields in

Smoke blackened the sky at a Standard Oil refinery in Richmond, California, around the turn of the 20th century.

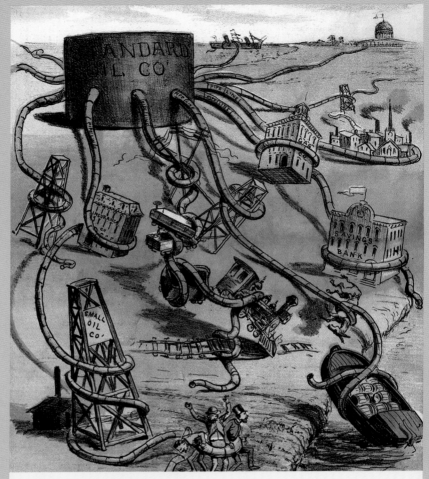

A political cartoon, titled "The Monster Monopoly," depicted Standard Oil as an octopus.

Ohio and Indiana. Rockefeller's trust bought almost all of these new properties. By 1891, although Standard Oil had owned no oil fields less than a decade before, it was producing 25 percent of America's crude oil.

Rockefeller's ruthlessness, however, was creating powerful enemies. His dominance of the industry would soon end.

Chapter 3

AUTOS SAVE THE OIL INDUSTRY

Thomas Edison perfected the first practical electric lightbulb in 1879. Before the end of the century, most American houses were lighted not by kerosene but by Edison's electric bulbs. The change threatened the fortunes of Rockefeller and the other oil tycoons.

But Henry Ford saved the oil business in 1900 when he launched the Detroit Automobile Company. Within months his first cars—powered by internal-combustion engines fueled by gasoline—began to appear on American roads. Between 1900 and 1910, more than half a million cars were sold in the United States. The demand for gasoline—and for the oil from which it was produced—soared. Existing oil fields could not supply the demand. Prospectors began searching for oil in unlikely places. They were often surly, uneducated men. They came to be called wildcatters, in part because of their unpredictable nature, and in part because of the wildcats they shot while clearing locations. They hung the wildcats' bodies from the oil derricks, and the wells became known as wildcat wells.

One wildcatter was a merchant named Patillo Higgins. He heard a story about a natural spring bubbling up out of a barren, salty hilltop called Spindletop in southeastern Texas near the town of Beaumont. Liquid from the spring occasionally caught on fire. Although experts thought oil fields were only in Eastern states, Higgins was convinced that oil could be found at the Spindletop site.

In 1900 Ohio produced more oil than any other state. Until then oil had been found almost exclusively near the

DANGER!

Work in the oil fields was extremely dangerous, and many men were killed there. Oil refineries blew up, oil tanks caught fire, and oil wells often and unexpectedly exploded and burst into flames. When an oil well is on fire, the fire is constantly fed from the oil below the surface, and it is very hard to put out. Nitroglycerin, an explosive, was sometimes used to try to stop the fires by blasting them, but this could, of course, make the fires worse. One reason "boom towns" got this nickname is that nitroglycerin often exploded in the town buildings where it was stored.

Great Lakes. Geologists were consulted about the Spindletop site. They proclaimed that the notion of finding oil anywhere near Beaumont was ridiculous.

But Higgins wasn't discouraged. He placed a newspaper ad for a professional oil well driller. Anthony Lucas, a salt and sulfur driller, was the only person who responded. Lucas examined the site and excitedly agreed with Higgins. They appealed to Standard Oil for help and were soundly rejected. It was one of the biggest mistakes John D. Rockefeller ever made.

A drilling crew posed at the Spindletop drill site in 1901.

"NODDING DONKEYS"

When wells are drilled and oil is found, it sometimes comes up under its own pressure. More often, however, it doesn't. The oil has to be pumped out of the ground. Oilmen nicknamed oil pumps "nodding donkeys" because of the way their driving beam (the "donkey's head") looks as if it were nodding up and down. As the "head" of the beam falls, the plunger enters the well. As the plunger rises, its suction draws oil to the surface.

Higgins and Lucas turned to Pittsburgh wildcatters James Guffey and John Galey, whose oil-prospecting adventures were financed by the Andrew Mellon family, the country's leading bankers. Guffey and Galey approached the Mellon brothers, who lent them $300,000 to lease about 15,000 acres (6,070 hectares) on and around Spindletop hill. Exploration could now begin.

Lucas began drilling in the fall of 1900. On January 10,

1901, the ground at Spindletop shook so hard that workers were nearly thrown off their feet. Then the well erupted, spewing oil high into the air at the rate of more than 100,000 barrels a day. It took nine days to bring the well under control. Before the gusher was capped, oil at the base of the hill created a lake a mile (1.6 kilometers) long. The Spindletop oil strike was the largest the world had ever seen.

The oil output at Spindletop was massive. This single find more than doubled total U.S. oil production, and it represented more than 15 percent of total world production. Immediately before the strike, land in the area was selling for

Oil at Spindletop came out of the ground in an enormous, high-pressure plume called a gusher. Today equipment at drill sites prevents such blowouts from occurring.

$10 an acre (0.4 hectares). Now a parcel that size was going for more than $1 million.

Almost overnight Beaumont grew from a town of 10,000 people to a city of 50,000. Dozens of rough and burly men were living in tents atop Spindletop. Gambling houses sprang up all over the city. An average of three murders took place each day. Beaumont became the home of not only hundreds of prostitutes, swindlers, and thieves, but also such extraordinarily wealthy families as the Mellons.

Oil derricks covered Spindletop hill, the site where oil was discovered in Texas. Today Texas is so renowned for its oil production that oil is sometimes called "Texas tea."

Andrew Mellon sent his younger brother, William, to manage the Spindletop property and to build an oil company that would compete with Rockefeller's Standard Oil. Spindletop was producing more than 3,000 barrels of oil an hour. William Mellon ordered construction of a pipeline 450 miles (724 km) long that would link Spindletop to the Mellon family's refinery at Port Arthur on the coast of the Gulf of Mexico. When the pipeline was completed, oil could be taken by ship to markets around the world. The Mellon oil company soon adopted the name Gulf Oil.

At about the same time, former Standard Oil pipeline supervisor Joe Cullinan set out on his own and founded the Texas Company. By 1905 he had bought some Beaumont oil wells and four large oil tankers, and he shortened the name of his company to Texaco.

An early 1900s advertisement for Texaco

The Story of OIL

The discovery of oil at Spindletop had led to the creation of Gulf Oil and Texaco, which became the first real competitors to Rockefeller's Standard Oil. Then Ida Tarbell, a pioneering investigative journalist, wrote *The History of the Standard Oil Company*. Published in 1904, the book exposed Rockefeller's ruthless tactics and their destructive effect on smaller businesses. Her exposé created powerful negative sentiment against Standard Oil. The result was a public outcry against the company so great that, after an investigation, the U.S. Supreme Court ruled in January 1911 that Standard Oil Trust had violated federal laws against restricting free trade. On May 15, the Supreme Court decreed that Standard Oil would have to be broken up. The company was so large that this resulted in the creation of 37 new oil companies.

A political cartoon suggested that Standard Oil's monopoly made Rockefeller the king of the world

THE HISTORY OF THE STANDARD OIL COMPANY

Ida Tarbell's *The History of the Standard Oil Company* was instantly popular with readers. Even though Tarbell described Rockefeller's unethical tactics in detail, sympathetically portraying Pennsylvania's independent oil workers, she was careful to recognize the perfection of the business structure he had created. She did not condemn capitalism itself, but rather "the open disregard of decent ethical business practices by capitalists." About the men of Standard Oil, she wrote, "They had never played fair, and that ruined their greatness for me."

Tarbell's book included a long and detailed character study of Rockefeller. "Our national life is on every side distinctly poorer, uglier, meaner, for the kind of influence he exercises," she concluded. Rockefeller was deeply hurt by this attack from "that poisonous woman," as he called her, but he refused to publicly defend himself against her claims. "Not a word," he told his advisers. "Not a word about that misguided woman."

The History of the Standard Oil Company made Ida Tarbell one of the most influential women in America. And it helped start a new form of writing that would eventually come to be called investigative journalism. In 1999 Tarbell's book was ranked fifth among the top 100 works of 20th century American journalism.

At 73 John D. Rockefeller retired and became a philanthropist. Although he had lived ruthlessly as a business owner, he founded the University of Chicago and the Rockefeller Institute for Medical Research, which is now New York City's Rockefeller University. His gift of $5 million to the U.S. government helped create Great Smoky Mountains National Park.

A 1923 advertisement for Mobil, which formed after the breakup of Standard Oil

The government-forced breakup of Standard Oil transformed the petroleum business into a competitive industry. Exxon, Mobil, and Chevron are all Standard Oil Company spin-offs. Fierce competition among these companies throughout the 20th century changed the nature of American life and helped make the United States the most powerful nation in the world.

THE TEAPOT DOME SCANDAL

One of the earliest and greatest scandals in American politics involved oil. The naval oil reserves were areas of oil-rich land that were set aside for the exclusive use of the U.S. Navy. But in 1921, Secretary of the Interior Albert Fall persuaded President Warren G. Harding to transfer control of the reserves in Elk Hills and Buena Vista, California, and Teapot Dome, Wyoming, to the Department of the Interior. Fall then rented the reserves in exchange for large sums of money paid to him personally. Word got out about Fall's unethical practices, which led to a Senate investigation that continued for several years. The investigation brought the corruption to light and made the scandal known as Teapot Dome the first symbol of government corruption in 20th century America.

Chapter 4

OIL FUELS GLOBAL CONFLICT

Throughout the 1900s—even during the Great Depression—the number of gasoline-powered cars on America's roads grew. During two world wars America dominated the global oil industry, a fact that was of immense help in winning the wars. The Allies beat the Nazis in Africa because the formidable German tank corps ran out of fuel deep in the Sahara desert.

From 1945 to 1950, the number of privately owned, gasoline-fueled vehicles in the United States grew from 26 million to 40 million. America's obsession with the automobile had become an addiction.

ATTENTION!

"Your work is vital to Victory... Our ships... Our planes... Our tanks *must* have oil!"

Stick to your job— **OIL IS AMMUNITION**

A World War II poster featuring General Dwight D. Eisenhower stressed oil's importance.

OIL AND WORLD WAR II

World War II began in 1939 in Europe, but it wasn't until Japan attacked the U.S. naval base at Pearl Harbor, Hawaii, in 1941 that the United States entered the conflict. What prompted Japan to attack the United States at Pearl Harbor? Japan's oil market was dominated by two Western companies. Japan knew that once it entered the war, the companies would cut off its oil supply. So Japan planned to attack the Dutch East Indies to gain control of the region's oil reserves. The United States, however, was aware of Japan's plans, and it positioned its fleet at Pearl Harbor in case Japan moved against the Indies.

To attack the Indies, Japan knew, it needed to first weaken the U.S. naval forces, which it accomplished with its December 7 attack. Japan went on to take over the oil fields in the Dutch East Indies. But the U.S. Navy sank most oil tankers leaving the Indies before they reached Japan. By 1944 Japan had cut back its military operations because of a lack of fuel.

By the start of the 1950s, American life had been changed forever by the automobile. People moved away from cities and lived miles from their workplaces in areas that came to be known as suburbs. A major sign of a person's success in the 1950s and 1960s was owning and driving a large, fast, powerful automobile.

After the war, a big car and a house in the suburbs became major parts of the American Dream.

FILL 'ER UP

In the 1950s and 1960s, as drivers drove their cars into gas stations, they were sometimes quickly and politely greeted by a team of station employees. The employees wore well-pressed uniforms with company patches on them and hats that looked like those worn by police officers. The team swarmed around the car, pumping the gas, cleaning front and back windshields, checking the car's levels of oil and transmission fluid and the water level in the radiator, as well as the tire pressure and the tread on each tire. The customer remained in the car and paid through the window only after these services were completed. (Self-service gas stations did not exist in the United States until the mid-1970s. Even today some states offer full-service only.) Customers who bought gas at the same station every week were often given merchandise rewards, such as dishes, glassware, sets of forks, knives and spoons, and entire cases of soda pop.

Throughout these years, dozens of huge oil companies battled for consumer business. Phillips Petroleum and other businesses sprang up from newly discovered oil fields in Oklahoma. International companies such as British Petroleum also became important in the oil business. In the United States, more than 20 large companies were selling the same products at roughly the same prices. Image and service became the ways these companies tried to create and keep customers who would use their products rather than those of the competition.

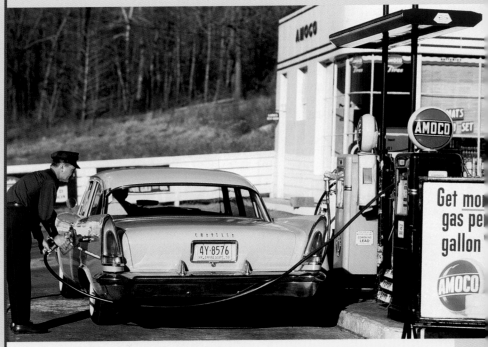

A filling-station attendant pumped gas into a new Chrysler at an Amoco station in 1958.

Dissatisfied with the ways American and British oil companies controlled the world market—keeping prices low by underpaying foreign oil producers—the leaders of Iran, Iraq, Kuwait, Saudi Arabia, and Venezuela met in Baghdad in 1960 and formed the Organization of Petroleum Exporting Countries. By the late 1960s, American oil fields could no longer meet domestic demand, and American consumers increasingly relied on foreign oil. At the same time, Middle

Representatives of Saudi Arabia met with delegates from other OPEC member countries at a meeting in the 1970s.

Eastern displeasure with the United States grew, as did the membership of OPEC. The group soon came to play an important role in controlling the supply of oil and influencing its price.

On October 6, 1973—which was Yom Kippur, the holiest day in the Jewish calendar—Egypt and Syria opened a coordinated surprise attack against Israel, which began the Yom Kippur War. At least nine Arab states, including four non-Middle Eastern nations, actively aided the Egyptian-Syrian war effort.

The Arab countries were swiftly resupplied by sea and air from the Soviet Union. As a result, the United States began airlifting supplies to Israel. On October 15, 1973, the 13 Arab nations of OPEC placed an oil embargo on the United States for its support of Israel. A week later the United Nations Security Council adopted a resolution that called on "all parties … to cease all firing and terminate all military activity immediately." The resolution ended the war.

It did not stop the embargo, however. Within weeks OPEC had almost completely halted oil exports to Western countries. And it had quadrupled the price of the oil that was sold. For the first time since the invention of the automobile, gasoline and oil products were suddenly in short supply in the United States. Many Americans thought the country might run out of oil.

A lot of service stations could not get gas from suppliers. Those that could get it sold it in small amounts. In early 1974, federally enforced gasoline rationing went into effect in the United States. Customers in most large American cities could buy gas only on certain days of the week, depending on the last number of their license plates. Service stations were open only a few hours a day, and customers had to wait in line—often a very long line—up to three hours to fill their tanks.

Shrinking oil production meant gas shortages and long lines at the pump during the 1970s.

The Story of **OIL**

This crisis prompted a request from the U.S. government for individuals and businesses to conserve energy. The United States Advertising Council created a public-service campaign around the slogan "Don't Be Fuelish." U.S. automobile manufacturers soon began making smaller cars. Japanese companies such as Toyota and Honda, whose cars were less expensive and used less gas, began to sell millions of automobiles in the United States. What's more, people began to insulate their homes better, and they adjusted their heating and cooling temperatures to use less oil. And for the first time, people began to talk about developing alternative energy sources, such as wind, solar, and nuclear energy, and natural gas.

As time passed, the OPEC oil embargo was lifted. Although supplies returned to normal, oil products were now much more expensive. Throughout the rest of the 1970s and 1980s, America and its economy were troubled by problems related to its reliance on oil from other countries.

Many oil companies drill offshore in search of new sources of domestic oil.

THE ARCTIC NATIONAL WILDLIFE REFUGE

If the United States is to continue its fossil-fuel-based economy, it needs to find low-cost oil within its borders. One proposal is to explore for oil in the Arctic National Wildlife Refuge. The ANWR covers about 19 million acres (7.7 million hectares) along Alaska's north coast, and it is home to large populations of caribou and other wildlife.

Environmentalists strongly object to any oil exploration in the region. They say drilling operations and pipelines could permanently destroy or disrupt wildlife in the area. Those who favor exploration say that from 5.5 billion to 16 billion barrels of crude oil and natural gas may be buried under the ANWR tundra, and that new methods of drilling can ensure that only a tiny part of the entire refuge would be disrupted. The battle between the two forces is one of the hottest political arguments over energy exploration in the developed world.

In August 1990, under the leadership of Iraq's dictator, Saddam Hussein, the Iraqi army invaded its oil-rich neighbor, Kuwait. Hussein claimed that Kuwait had been drilling into Iraqi oil fields and stealing Iraqi oil. Wanting to secure oil supplies and worried that Iraq would invade Saudi Arabia and gain control of its massive oil fields, the United States and several allies went to war against Iraq. It's estimated that more than 100,000 Iraqi civilians were killed during the 1990

Burning oil fields in Kuwait during 1990's Operation Desert Storm

Gulf War, and retreating Iraqi troops set fire to hundreds of Kuwaiti oil wells. After Iraq's defeat, oil prices and the U.S. economy again stabilized.

This was not the end of oil-related conflicts, however. In 2003 the United States invaded Iraq, which it claimed harbored terrorists and had weapons of mass destruction. Some people, however, argued that the claims were not true and that the real reason for the U.S. invasion was to protect global oil supplies. If the United States could remove Saddam Hussein and install a friendly regime, they said, that would keep oil cheap and flowing freely.

Though a new government was installed, the U.S. occupation caused a disruption in oil production. Since 2002 oil prices have increased 400 percent. Furthermore, no weapons of mass destruction were found.

By the start of the new millennium, the global dominance enjoyed by U.S. oil companies throughout most of the 20th century had ended. In the early 21st century, America's obsession with, and addiction to, oil products is becoming recognized as unhealthful and not something that can continue.

☐ Chapter 5

OIL ALL AROUND US

Oil isn't just the source of the gasoline that powers our vehicles and the lubricant that keeps their many parts moving. Nor is it simply the fuel that heats our homes in winter. Not by a long shot.

Look around you right now. The steering wheel, accelerator and brake pedals, the floor mats, the console, and the seats you're sitting on in your car or school bus have parts made from oil. So do the plastic seats of your school desks. The same is true of the plastic bowl you ate your cereal from this morning, as well as the plastic-coated wrap that kept the cereal fresh inside its box. Oil is what the casings of your pens and mechanical pencils are made from. And your cell phone, your computer, and your iPod are made in large part from oil products. The cover of this book you're reading is stiffened and made shiny by products derived from oil. The stretch material in your jeans and T-shirts is made from oil. Even the soles of your shoes and the elastic in the waistband of your underwear are created from oil.

Many everyday items are made, at least in part, from oil.

These materials are made from petrochemicals, which are chemical products made from petroleum or other fossil fuels. Ethylene and acetylene are two petrochemicals used to create plastics, synthetic fabrics, adhesives, and paints. Many of the major oil companies have petrochemical divisions, and other large corporations are involved in petrochemicals.

The petroleum industry is the world's largest and most varied business. Almost no matter where you're sitting or standing, oil-based products are all around you, everywhere you can see.

These products have enriched and brought pleasure to our lives. Over the past 100 years, oil has allowed us to have a level of comfort and luxury that has never before existed. Much of this is now starting to change. That's because many scientists estimate that at the rate we now use fossil fuels, the world's reserves will last only 40 to 70 more years.

Another reason to change is to prevent oil-induced harm to the environment. Oil spills pollute rivers, bays, seas, and oceans, killing millions of animals and plants. Fuel particles in the air we breathe cause allergies, heart disease, and cancer.

Oil spills claim the lives of birds and marine animals and threaten the health of humans.

THE *EXXON VALDEZ* OIL SPILL

One of the biggest environmental problems related to oil has been spills from huge tanker ships used to transport oil around the world. The most famous of these took place in 1989, when the tanker *Exxon Valdez* hit an Alaskan reef. The 12 million gallons (45.4 million liters) of oil it was carrying leaked out and spread along 1,200 miles (1,930 km) of undeveloped coastline. To get a picture of how much oil this is, it's enough to fill nearly 1,000 Olympic-size swimming pools with sticky black oil.

The oil from the *Exxon Valdez* killed more than 250,000 sea birds (including birds of several endangered species), 2,800 sea otters, 300 seals, and thousands of other animals. It also killed countless millions of fish and other marine animals and greatly damaged a formerly beautiful coastline. It was the largest and deadliest oil spill in American history, but sadly only the 35th worst spill worldwide.

The worst result of worldwide oil use, though, may be global warming. Al Gore, a former vice president of the United States and Nobel Peace Prize winner, has called global warming "the most significant challenge human beings have ever faced." In 2009 it was determined that the extinction rate resulting from human-caused climate change is greater than it was during the mass extinction that killed the dinosaurs 75 million years ago. Many scientists all over the world are sure that chemicals released into Earth's atmosphere by the daily burning of petroleum products threaten the very existence of life on our planet. Burned petroleum products are putting so much extra carbon dioxide into the

Oil refineries and power plants that burn fossil fuels are among the primary causes of global warming.

planet's atmosphere that they are quickly making the world a much warmer place. Carbon dioxide is one of the gases responsible for the greenhouse effect, which causes global warming by trapping heat close to the planet's surface.

One of the first things that will happen because of global warming is the melting of the ice caps in Antarctica and the Arctic. This is why the polar bear, the emperor penguin, and many other animals are in trouble. Furthermore, as the polar

Global warming is causing polar ice to melt, affecting ocean levels worldwide.

ice caps melt, coastal cities of the world will flood, including New York City, Washington, D.C., Los Angeles, Miami, San Francisco, London, Tokyo, Beijing, Venice, and Sydney. Hundreds of islands around the world will disappear into the ocean.

While the coastal areas are flooding, other areas of the world will be drying up because of global warming. Huge chunks of China, India, Europe, Canada, and the United States are expected to become deserts.

The greenhouse effect and global warming not only superheat the air, but they pump it so full of energy that the world's climate is getting much stormier. There are now many more hurricanes and tornadoes than there were just a few decades ago, and these storms are bigger and more severe than they used to be.

With each day, it's becoming increasingly obvious that we need to move away from petroleum products as the fuel for our vehicles, our homes, and the economy of our planet. How can this be accomplished? Scientists are working to develop automobiles and trucks that have zero emissions. Car companies are already manufacturing—and consumers are buying—hybrid automobiles that combine a gasoline-burning engine with an electric motor.

Many people believe that a switch to renewable resources is the best solution. Clean, renewable energy can be made using the sun, wind, water, plants, and Earth's internal heat. These sources could create enough energy to heat, cool, and power homes and workplaces. And the technology is being developed to create all-electric plug-in cars and trucks that are powered by energy from the wind and the sun. Renewable energy is becoming increasingly available and affordable.

Wind turbines convert the movement of air—a clean, renewable resource—into electrical power.

In addition to developing renewable sources of energy, there's much we can easily do to reduce our dependence on oil and decrease greenhouse gas emissions. Instead of driving cars, people can take trains, streetcars, and buses, which, on average, use half to one-third as much energy per person. In the United States, fewer than 5 percent of people travel in these ways. That's the lowest percentage of mass-transit use of any industrialized nation. If only 10 percent of Americans used public transportation daily, the country's greenhouse emissions would be reduced by more than 25 percent.

What's more, people can buy food that's grown and harvested locally. Most of the food eaten in the United States has traveled hundreds or thousands of miles by truck, airplane, or train to get to the stores. People can save enormous amounts of oil simply by buying from farmers markets, where the food that is sold has been grown on nearby farms or in neighbors' gardens.

At home and at work, people can use much less energy by setting their thermostats one or two degrees lower in the winter and one or two degrees higher in the summer. Turning off unused lights also reduces energy consumption, as does switching off computers instead of leaving them on standby. Even more helpful is replacing traditional incandescent lightbulbs with the latest, most efficient compact fluorescent bulbs, which use 80 percent less energy.

With oil resources dwindling and the public becoming more aware of the dangers of using petroleum products, the sun seems to be setting on the story of oil.

These are only a few examples of the many things that can be done now by each of us to use less oil at little to no sacrifice in the quality of our lives. The story of oil is long, powerful, and dramatic. Because it appears to be drawing to a close, we must find a way to give it the happiest of possible endings.

The Story of OIL

Timeline

1849 Abraham Gesner discovers how to separate crude oil into various parts, including kerosene, diesel, and gasoline

1854 Gesner creates the North American Kerosene Gas Light Company

1859 Edwin L. Drake discovers oil in Pennsylvania

1864 John D. Rockefeller buys his first oil refinery

1870 Rockefeller forms Standard Oil Company

1891 Standard Oil produces 25 percent of America's crude oil

1900 Henry Ford launches the Detroit Automobile Company, creating a new demand for oil products; Ohio is the largest oil-producing state

1901 Oil is discovered at Spindletop near Beaumont, Texas; Andrew Mellon founds Gulf Oil; Joe Cullinan founds Texas Company, later called Texaco

1911 U.S. Supreme Court rules that Standard Oil must be broken up; 37 new companies are created as a result